I WILL OFFEND YOU

PART II

EMAN ALJAROUDI

CONTENTS

DEDICATION

To anyone who ever thought 'who am I?'
to even try something like that and then
went ahead and did it anyway.

To my beautiful family and friends.

To my beloved nephew & neice, Malik & Medina.

PART

I

Seven life lessons with
random explanations

I love you, and because I love you, I would
sooner have you hate me for telling you the
truth than adore me for telling you lies.

Pietro Aretino

1. DON'T LISTEN AND RUN

Everyone wants to be heard. To be important. To be substantial and worthwhile.

What about you? Are you like everyone? Whose dream do you chase or build? Your own or your boss's dream? What mark are you leaving behind?

Do you even care or is the idea of being a sheep inoffensive to you because you went to Europe that summer one time on a Contiki tour and now you're cultured? You probably came back and unpacked your bags, looked at your 500 new Instagram posts of you eating pizza in every village and city that makes up Italy and concurred that the 50 or so likes you got was enough reward for your new cultured self.

So you go back to the same day job you've hated for the last 10 years, even though you specifically told Samantha whats-her-face on the back of the Contiki bus that when you came back you would quit that damned Satan spawn of a job, and tell Martha, your fat slob of a boss, that you want to be an art curator in Venice like you have always dreamed of and marry Dimitri, the tourist shop owner's son.

But you don't and you hate yourself. Not a bad reason to hate yourself, hey?

Here's some truth. Healthy people with self-respect will not tolerate your empty promises (if they have a backbone) and you think that your subconscious mind does? You think you can cheat yourself of an absolutely beautiful, limitless, sensational life because you can lie to you and think there are no repercussions?

Think again dumb-dumb. Yeah, I called you dumb-dumb. Let's sort it out.

You will take things from this book and I will refer to random explanations and stories and it will be up to you to take the bits and pieces that sing to you and run with them.

No legacy is so rich as honesty.

William Shakespeare

2. LISTEN UP

Listen up.

Life doesn't care about your whining. Life doesn't care about the guy or girl or trans-whatever human who cheated on you and now you don't eat cheese because it reminds you of him.

Life doesn't give you value if you don't give yourself value so stop feeling sorry for yourself. It's unbecoming. Don't treat yourself like a bystander and follow through on more promises to Harry the fat cat across the road than you do to yourself. Don't say, 'Harry, I'm going to treat you to some John West olive blend tuna.' Then follow through and get Harry the tuna if you wouldn't do the same thing for yourself.

I'm not saying go find someone called Dimitri and leave your world at a drop of a dime, I'm saying make the promises and agreements you make to yourself just as important as the ones you make to another human, such as Harry.

This might come as a surprise, but you are just another human, and the way you treat yourself is a reflection of what you agree to tolerate in life. You need a genuine self-love contract between yourself and however many personalities you have along with you, comprende? Good. Let's continue.

There is nothing more dignified than a corpse.

Evan Esar

3. RUIN YOURSELF BY YOURSELF

We all crave affection unless you are a serial killer and oxytocin isn't your thing.

So when the suitor we want comes along with the right pheromones and hairstyle we go ahead and pretend it's perfectly fine to act like a prepubescent teenager and fall into the medical term called the 'love fart'. These love farts are so intense that they knock the wind right out of you.

Love farts happen to the best of us. The issue arises when our sensory acuity receptor focuses on nothing but them and then scarcity kicks in because you will never find a John Mathew III with genetics, a moustache and broad shoulders to protect you from wild bears like him in your life.

It's better to feel like you can U-Haul all your unresolved daddy issues and childhood trauma onto this person you met five seconds ago and what tops that is that you've already managed to sniff his hair. If this is not how you behave or how anyone has ever behaved towards you then throw this book out your window, but first set it on fire.

Now let's delve into this scarcity and self-loathing, you know, the thing that's ruining your bloody chance at anything close to a relationship of any sort with healthy boundaries. And what the hell are boundaries?

Your clinginess and neediness ruins good opportunities because a stable relationship with your current partner (ie. Tom) is too boring and you can't stand that he speaks to you with respect. Instead, you want Marcus the tatted-up third generation biker gang member who doesn't even acknowledge your existence to give you a healthy dose of hate that you subconsciously think you deserve.

Did I say that out loud? Did I make something tingle? If I did, you got some real internal searching that needs to stop sliding under the rug, and no, another Shiraz won't make it go away.

Nothing is at last sacred but the
integrity of your own mind.

Ralph Waldo Emmerson

4. WHO CONTROLS THIS PLACE?

What controls your focus? How much of your attention is stolen because you let yourself be persuaded so easily?

There is so much that is fighting for your attention that you're not sure your newborn deserves all of it. Do you doubt what I just said or do you not have a newborn so you don't care because it's not about you? Is it ever not about you? If it had nothing to do with you would you care?

On another selfish note what about an awkward conversation on a date? Can you stand the heat or be frank and kind enough to let the poor sod know he's got no chance because he doesn't know how to salsa in the moonlight with you and you can't live with someone who can't.

Do you think of a way to run? You know, the usual 'Whoops, my friend's cat needs a bath and well, you know, I have a mum so I really have to run but it's been great and let's never do this again. Bye!"

You run and do nothing social. You just jump on your Facebook feed and how interesting is it to scroll and not care about any of it except for that one photo of you that you're tagged in three years ago where you're so skinny.?

You scroll some more and you find Jennifer, your ex-best friend from high school, down in Africa helping children build a well for fresh water, and you're triggered. 'Really, Jennifer, if you did it out of your own genuine esteem you wouldn't post about it for attention!' But you like and comment anyway because who needs honesty and integrity anymore?

You say one thing and do another. Is it so brutal to be honest? To have someone's absolute attention and trust and tell them what you really think or feel? Is it so obscure and downright weird? Do you even want anyone's absolute attention? So much attention and love...

Can you take two steps back and let me want you? For God's sake, we've only been dating for two years! You say, 'This is going way too fast for me, I can't be tied down.' What? You don't think so?

'Well, I can't possibly confront or talk about my deep underlying issues of being in a committed relationship so I'm just going to say we go ahead and start dating other people so that I can repeat this cycle with the next person who falls my way. Don't worry, I'll make sure my friends know you are way too clingy. It's been fun, Ciao. Good riddance.'

Funny that everyone else seems to have these issues and you're always the normal one. It's definitely them because you have this comforting story that you tell yourself to boost your ego and also your mum loves you.

How long will you hide in your stories? How unfulfilled and empty will you make yourself and others until you decide to look to the creator of every decision you have ever made? Yes, you dumb-dumb. Always look inwardly, never outwardly.

The strongest love is the love that
can demonstrate its fragility.

Paulo Coelho

5. SHUN THE 'V' WORD

Vulnerability. To open yourself so bravely, so boldly and make it a mark of how you live your life. Did you say it scared you? To have all those walls you worked so hard to build come down in the name of… what did you call it again? Love?

Heck no, you won't allow it. Why? Love is giving all of you. Not getting. It's not about you. However, even knowing this you find yourself putting up this wall because you're making it all about you again.

It's at this point you start telling your best friend that you doubt his true masculine love for you and you're not 'feeling it' anymore. You fail to make the connection that you have retracted every means of letting your partner make any emotional connection with you by not letting them feel wanted or desired by the very thing they yearn for.

Get off your high horse and give of yourself.

Your partners are not mind readers, so if you expected them to know that when you said 'no' you really meant 'yes' because you made that face, you're asking for trouble. Why are you so hell-bent on running scared or putting up the Great Wall of China against people who can add so much beauty and value to your life?

When we feel so deeply in our bones, so instinctively in our gut that this person can be the twin flame of our lives, yet the scars left behind by Rachael (your previous love interest) cheating on you gives you a good enough reason to go running the opposite direction from Amy (your current love interest) who loves you blindly. Any time Amy gets a little too close for comfort you shut off.

Then what? You do what any emotionally wounded person does who's unwilling to work on growing from personal life experiences. You projectile shoot Amy right out of your achy breaky heart because you don't think she'll understand. Heck, you don't even understand.

My dear dumb-dumb, you must understand you and all your inner corners. Look into what hurts within your soul, listen to it, feed it, and you will blossom to life. As you blossom, you'll come to realise that nihilism and self-centeredness is the demise of sincere and honest love so focus your life on things outside yourself because you will always feel the most pain when you are all about you and no one else. If you don't like people, then give back to Mother Earth and plant a goddamn tree or something.

No, but really, I sincerely urge you to move on from that nihilistic standpoint. Tell the truth and open your heart. Love penetrates all. Give and you will get.

When you realise the value of life, you
dwell less on what is past and concentrate
more on the preservation of future.

Dian Fosse

6. THE 'HELP ME' FACTOR

Sometimes life doesn't go our way. That's inevitable. We lose our jobs, we lose our partners, we lose our money, we lose our cat, and we almost always lose our marbles.

But you can't expect to binge watch every Netflix series with your next door neighbour's cat and a bag of Doritos so that you don't have to take ownership of your life and avoid the many successes gifted to those who do something about it.

When you don't use a muscle you most definitely lose it, so create a connection to your passions in your mind. Don't get me wrong, it's healthy to heal by replacing a negative action with something healthier. For example, give up your self-centred, takes-selfies-of-his-body-in-a-bathroom-type boyfriend and replace him with a new gym membership and a somewhat healthy drooling aptitude for Arnold Schwarzenegger's biceps.

However, losing your marbles and then going ahead and lowering your consciousness in sappy unrealistic Netflix drama is what I call a double negative—it places you at the lower end of the food chain and you will be eaten. By what, you ask? Life will eat you, dumb-dumb.

So cut it out. Distraction will not give your life significance. Be outrageous, change your patterns of self-sabotage, and identify your tendency to do so. Teach your brain and see all the beautiful things you miss out on when you don't get up and pick the highest lemon on the tallest tree of your life. Yes, this is the part when I say, on cue, when life gives you lemons you damn well better make some Beyoncé-inspired lemonade.

Yes, I heard you when you said your upbringing wasn't perfect. You were used, abused, treated badly, reused, tossed to the side and lost a fuse or two or three. But let me ask you this, what is it that you expect of yourself? I can tell you from experience that everything in life comes down to choices. Are you going to sink or swim?

Two guys come back from war-torn Syria. One spends every day thinking about his losses and eventually shoots himself in the head. The other uses the emotion from the madness to propel himself forward and develop several projects in order to promote peace. Same experience; different outcomes. What's the key? MINDSET. What you associate with pleasure or pain in your mind is what you will get. In short, master your mind because everything is a state of mind. Know and master this and you will forever master your life.

I hoped we never had to realise all the
opportunities we missed in this life.

Elizabeth Berg

7. DO YOU HAVE TO DIE?

Where's your faith, dumb-dumb? Do you have to die to realise how precious life really is?

What aspect of your life is most important to you? The first thought that came to mind as soon as you read that sentence. For the few of you who had nothing come to mind, I'll just assume you're dead.

What if I took it away the aspect of your life that makes it worth living? (Does it actually make your life worth living?) What do you do when shit hits the fan and Jenny (from *The Block*) says, 'My boyfriend is my everything.' Somewhere along the line she stops yoga, she stops playing I Spy, she stops all the things that used to make her who she is so she can stay at home and make sandwiches for Jim (boyfriend).

Meanwhile, Jenny's everything is at the strippers every Tuesday paying ten dollars for a stripper called Candy to suck his toe. There's no honesty in the relationship considering that Jenny doesn't even know Jim has a toe fetish. Jenny walks in on this phalange session (details of how she got there not provided), comes in mid-toe-suck, loses her mind and gruesomely murders the perpetrators and then herself, and I mean blood everywhere.

What I am trying to highlight here is that had Jenny not believed that Jim was her whole existence, she, without a doubt, would not have been so quick to think her whole life wasn't worth living when she saw the betrayal unfold. This leads us to the fact that everything is relative to your perspective. How you think, what you feel, and how you react is all within your control and no matter how badly you think you lose everything, you never truly do lose everything unless… can we get a drum roll… YOU LOSE YOURSELF.

Your everything can be nothing in a split second, and God, it hurts. But here's the beauty—life is made of a multitude of facets and aspects and moments and joys and if you were present enough for two seconds instead of checking Instagram for the fifth time in five seconds (nothing's changed, no one likes you because you're self-deluded and #addicted to looking for happiness outside yourself).

Take a moment to take in the million other beautiful aspects of life that we so very often take for granted. That one loss is a pin drop in the ocean of possibility called your life. Open yourself to it and stop trying to bloody control everything. Just let go, be free, tune into the moment.

Stop playing games. Don't bullshit yourself or others. Manipulation is a sucker's sport and if you're into sucking, you'd better be prepared to suck like you came to lose. Because you will.

Gratitude and acceptance are NOT spiritual ways to live your life. Their way is to make sure your ego's on a leash and your authentic self comes through.

Be one of those individuals who have ridiculous passions and inspire the masses. Realise the power in being true to no one other than you, because nothing is more freeing than the truth. Free yourself, have courage, and never forget to be sassy in the process. It won't be easy, but it will be worth it. I love you, dumb-dumb.

We are done here.
Don't be offended. If you want more keep reading.

PART II

More lessons

Here we are again.
Face to face, yet I could only hope you have even read
the first part of this book. If you haven't you probably
should, but some of you probably won't and that's
fine for I will not be offended. You, however, well…

There may be fairies, there may be elves, but
God helps those who help themselves.

Stephen King

8. TILL DEATH DO WE PART

The world is misery. Deal with it

For what it's worth, don't cry me a river. Now, to be and truly feel substantial and worthwhile in the world is so very easy and we can all do it if we hold hands and wish for total world peace... In your dreams.

You want the truth? It takes hard work, guts, determination and, most of all, strong inner core values to feel truly substantial. To be substantial means never being complacent; never selling yourself short for short-term pleasures. It means you always see the end goal of who you want to be, or at the very least, see and envision the kind of person you can look at and not want to vomit. That's what we're dealing with here, to be quite frank, or Mary, or even bloody Donald trump.

So many people wake up and think not another goddamned day at this damned workplace or with this damned spouse and these dammed ADHD kids who don't even have ADHD. Do not lie to yourself. When shit hits the fan, you're inclined and even most welcome to think to yourself that everyone can all piss right off. But then reality sets in and you know you can't do any of that because you are deeply entangled in a web of responsibility, so much responsibility that will never set you free, and you can't breathe and, more dangerously, you think you can never get out. You are the hamster running on the wheel and you can't stop.

So you lose your mind (this might be the mid-whatever crisis happening). You leave your workplace that makes you unhappy, leave your spouse that makes you unhappy, throw your kids away or send them back to where they came from. You chug down that Pina Colada, you run off to Venice to be swept away in a bout of unimaginable romance and passion with your newfound love Dimitri or Dimitria.

Six months pass and you begin to resent Dimitri/Dimitria. You see how much your previous partner did for you. You see how being a waitress for tips in Venice is not as amusing and charming as it initially seemed. You notice how Venice, in all its beauty, is bland and it no longer feels as exciting and inviting as it did. You yearn to go back. You regret having made all those choices. You fly back. You thought you ran from it all but the responsibility ran with you. The responsibility of your choices will always run with you.

You see now that no choice we ever make is free of consequences. All choices bear a consequence no matter how big or small the choice. In your lifetime you will have so many choices to make. These choices will eventually shape you because what follows is their repercussions which invite opportunities, lovers, kids, Ferraris, wealth, poverty, sickness, addiction, yoga, Donald Trump being elected. These choices invite the world you want, and if you ever think that you didn't want that thing in my life, unfortunately, you did.

They determine who you become as a person because you will be afflicted with life's different character types—highs and lows that will ultimately shape your personality for better or worse. They will play out their purpose and either stay or leave after you have been dealt the card that resulted from the choices you made and actions you took whether you like it or not. Fortunately, for you, dumb-dumb, your only option is to make no choices ever, close all your blinds and have no friends and no life and rot in a corner. Wait, no. There is something else, actually—making good choices.

For the most part, the choices we make are made in terms of what's good or bad. And as the great Shakespeare said, 'for there is nothing either good or bad, but thinking makes it so '. While that statement has its merit, we must always consider that all truths are but half-truths.

Essentially, to some outlandish degree, that statement could blur lines for the following to occur— ridiculous displays of Romeo and Juliet type of love and threesomes with married couples, which I have no doubt are appearing. It could also constitute a statement such as, 'I'm currently a meth addict. However, I have a law degree and I'm just living a balanced life.' That statement is usually supported by some incredulous hipster statement such as, 'I'm into the nuances of being an educated drug addict, you know. Don't kill my vibe.'

No, I don't know, dumb-dumb, and I am here to kill your vibe by telling you that you will kill your own vibe because whenever you don't want to kill your 'vibe' you ride the free train of life devoid of responsibility. That leads you to the magical land of nowhere fast. Why is this, you ask? Well, my sweet darling dumb-dumb, it is because the end result of your choices is never in mind. It is always that devilishly sweet temptation of the moment that devours and ruins one too many a soul. So let me ask you this—are you willing to cave in for a taste?

The road to hell is paved with good intentions. However, all a good choice requires is for you to think. But at what cost? If you are willing to wear that cost—rob the supermarket, run the streets naked, tell your boss in your best French what you really think of his leadership style. Don't ever be unhappy with the consequence if you're willing to wear it. Well, you can be, but that's your choice because yes, you'll wear whatever being unhappy gives you.

You are who you are today and for the rest of your life because it's what you wanted. You'd be wisest to sink your teeth into the opportunities that bring you closest to the truth—opportunities that rid the world of suffering—but first, it's best to start with trying to make amends with that ridiculous self-fulfilling prophecy of yours.

Whether you think you can, or you can't, you're right.

Henry Ford

9. CAN YOU FULFILL MY PROPHECY?

What self-fulfilling prophecy did I mean? What is a self-fulfilling prophecy? Broadly speaking, it is the notion that whatever you believe will happen will actually happen. Then, without fail, you're so crushed and upset when you bloody damn well knew what the outcome would be anyway. Dumb-dumb, miracles don't happen. Well, they might, but it's best not to rely on them.

For those of you who think this is some hippy mind programming stuff, think again. I will show you truth. You ought to know full well that whatever you believe in your mind has a massive impact on how you conduct yourself as a person and, more importantly, the body language that you display.

It's long been said that actions speak louder than words and, as humans, we are, from an evolutionary standpoint, inclined to believe a person's behaviour as opposed to the words they are speaking. If their words and behaviour don't line up, we are immediately on our guard because we see an incongruent individual who, in our minds, seems manipulative or, at the very least, becomes an untrustworthy individual with no backbone. As a result, we immediately reject them or, as the famous mean girls would say, 'You can't sit here!'

So when you walked up to the girl/boy/ant that you fancy and you fill yourself with whatever courage you can find—liquid, drug or natural—and you think in your mind, 'I hope she doesn't reject me', I hate to break it to you, dumb-dumb, but they will most probably reject you. Mainly because you anticipated it. Your mind absorbed it, your body attuned to it by being weak and feeble, and your approach to your future lover was all but charming and witty. It was weak, incongruent and, as a result, in-authentic.

You wanted one thing but you anticipated something else and you put yourself at a crossroads that made you unsure of what you wanted. Furthermore, this came out in your body language, which meant that your love interest most definitely picked up on this unsure decision to ask them out, that is if they have any social acuity.

Now tell me truthfully—why the hell would you give someone a chance to break your heart if their first approach to you is one of weakness, especially if they seem so unsure if they even want you? For God's sake, why would you even waste your time? Most won't. Instead, they will wait for someone who means what they say and says what they mean. Do you know what I mean?

If you can manage to not doubt the faith you have in yourself and know what you want and go for it, you're more likely to get what you want. This is all within reason, of course. And, once again all truths are but half-truths. You win some, you lose some. But trust this, dumb-dumb, you will respect yourself more when your words match your actions and, as a result, others will respect you more too. Unless you're into the trend of self-sabotage.

I craft my own tragedies without ever having
even the remotest understanding that it is
I myself who have done the crafting.

Craig D Lounsbrough

10. SABOTAGE ME, PLEASE

Ah, our good old friend self-sabotage. I'm sure most of us have heard or are experts in this particular field. Some could even win a Nobel Prize for being so fantastic at self-sabotaging.

I know you're thinking—'Yeah, but self-sabotage has helped me so many times by letting me not get my hopes up too high about that relationship, that job, that whatever meaningful thing that means a lot to me.' Not getting it means you've been saved from the ridicule of the possibility, plus that person who you thought was hot is no longer hot so you're also saved from a non-vain relationship with a non-hot person.

This self-sabotage doesn't occur as a defence mechanism. It occurs because you subconsciously program your mind with poisonous affirmations like 'I'll never truly amount to anything' or 'I don't truly deserve it', 'that lecturer was right, I am nothing' or 'Mum and Dad are right, there's no future in that career'. And, the all-time winner, 'That opinionated nurse, Kim, was right—my arse does look fat in these jeans.'

I understand; they were mean and they don't understand you, which for the most part, is true, but you must understand this selfish act they did has nothing to do with you. They reflected their ideals onto you and, to add some lemon to your paper cut, they said some condescending bullshit like 'it's for your own good'.

It wasn't a particularly fun time but here's the thing—they may have said these words but you are the master of your own reality until you're dead and then I'm not sure what happens. For most individuals for whom this hits home, you can take it that step further when you let their selfish ideals affect you. When you let their words permeate through your mind and your soul, you give yourself permission to believe these things. It may not always be on the surface level but, more dangerously, on a deeper, more subconscious level.

So we turn to the mind—the self-chatter, the mini-me, the compadre, the voice that talks in your head when not required and also finds that strangers backside nice to look at in those jeans, even though your partner and one year old are right beside you. Then just as we would look at the quality of the food we eat, the quality of the way we dress, the quality of the phone we buy, we also need to look at the quality and validity of the thoughts that create so much noise in our minds.

How we perceive ourselves is imperative, if not essential, to our mental outlook and, in turn, how we perceive the world will treat us and how generously it's willing to give to us. As James Allen says, 'You are today where your thoughts have brought you, you are today where your thoughts take you'. For many, their thoughts and imagination play a vital role in how successful they are.

However, if we step away from that idea and consider that we are not our thoughts and our thoughts are not us, we are able to focus on what is directly in front of us. When we are able to focus our attention on what is in front of us we can be present with whatever needs our attention in the given moment.

Your unnecessary thoughts are in charge of the self-sabotage you bestow on yourself. The less you identify with your thoughts, the more you are able to use intuition to guide you, the less you react, the less you assume, and the less you stress about the things that happened previously or have not yet happened. In the place of not listening to that incessant chatter in your head, you are stripped of thoughts and expectations, and you just get to be. Now you can master yourself and take on the world because you can be you. Breathe; it feels nice.

Your beliefs go hand in hand with the action you take. However, the action must be taken with focus, clarity and a silent mind. A silent mind can only be achieved through disconnection from useless thoughts and instead, feeling the natural intuition that we instinctively have but rarely use.

It must also be noted that if you take a strong belief but no pencil to paper, you lose. If you take action but have no belief or vision in what you're trying to accomplish, you lose. So you can begin to see why you would lose if you have one and not the other—your will propels you to keep going when the going gets tough. However, if your mind is not right if it is filled with distracting, negative thoughts that you identify with because you assume your thoughts are you. Then you'll surely give up the moment things start to get hairy or, at the very least, get frustrated and punch the old lady passing you in the street. Not good.

To take action with no clear vision of the end goal means your effort isn't focused so it is scattered, which makes you less effective. This makes it much more difficult and requires more energy and time to achieve what you want.

If you take an axe to take down a big tree, and you begin hacking in different places you'll make plenty of dents, but not enough to bring the tree down. However, if you continuously hack at the same position, with enough patience and consistent effort you will bring that tree down.

What am I saying here? Focused effort, a silent mind, dis-identification with your thoughts and planned action is the key to success within one's self and, in turn, in whatever it is you wish to accomplish. As always, this is all within reason—do not go ahead and focus your efforts on trying to make Brad Pitt or Angelina Jolie your potential partner, thinking you have created a focused effort and a plan of action to make them love you and have them re-enact scenes from *Mr and Mrs*

Smith with you, then hello, hello they're suddenly yours. No, dumb-dumb. And it's not a limiting belief either. Some things in life are not meant for us and as with everything in life, we need to learn to be reasonable, patient and move on when necessary.

Avoid going into your head and wishing situations were different. That game is futile and you will never win. Dumb-dumb, you must face yourself and face the things you don't like about yourself so you don't end up resenting who you are as an individual. I understand that it might be easier to wish you were born into a different life, saying things like, 'Man, Josh the captain of the soccer team is so cool. I wish I was like him. My life would be so much better.' Or, more commonly, 'I wish I was more like Barbie. She's hairless and beautiful and I have a moustache. She doesn't even have to try to be intelligent because she gets what she wants anyway.'

Barbie's shit, but to an obscure degree, that plastic thing is actually respected. If a plastic thing can get respect and love, then you damn well better believe you can. Always know that you are worthy of all the things that you can offer to others and it is you who must be willing to give before you can truly appreciate what you receive.

If people keep stepping on you, wear a pointy hat.

Joyce Rachelle

11. JUST A SIDE OF PUSH ME OVER

No one likes a pushover. In saying that, you most definitely don't have to be an aggressive bulldozer, but, as I mentioned earlier, you do need to respect yourself and give others the same reason to respect you. Remember this, dumb-dumb, you are everything you think you are and you are everything you think you're not, and the only person who can change that is you.

You are the end and the beginning of whatever life you want. You must know and accept this because it's the only way you can start hacking at the goals you want for your life or, at the very least, it's the only way you can begin to like yourself.

I get it—you don't know where to start and, depending on your situation, what you need to do can vary to a great extent. However, if you can note the type of person, personality traits and core values that appeal to you—that you would respect—note them down. Keep them in your mind and heart and when shit hits the fan, let those traits hold you together. Know that you have those traits to fall back on as oppose to the approval of a mere individual who probably doesn't give a rat's arse about you anyway, or maybe they do, but it doesn't matter.

You need to be your own saviour; you must know this. Seeking approval from others for the person you are instead of knowing who you are and seeking nothing but wisdom will hurt you. It weakens you and most definitely keeps you from finding who you truly want to be. Undoubtedly, you will stay lost, you will stay approval seeking and incongruent. You will stay that person who no one really wants around but they invite you out of pity. Is that the life you want?

If it is, then stop reading. I don't want you to read this because it's not for you and you'd best give it to someone who wants to set boundaries so that people can not readily shit all over them at will. Someone who wants to have an inner direction and core values so that they can hold it together and not break down and cry when someone says they smell and look like they've been hit by the ugly stick. More importantly, they can hold it together and be a source of strength when everyone else is breaking down around them.

There's true value in being able to hold your own and you'll find a significance in your life that you never knew was there when you can go within to find strength and abundance rather than relying on other people's approval. You, my darling, need to approve of yourself.

Approving of yourself will get you places and give you a life of your own. However, approving of yourself means coming from a place of abundance in every interaction you have in your existence. Now you're thinking, 'What the hell is this place of abundance that I need to come from and why would it get me anything? Is it Narnia?' No, dumb-dumb, it's not in Narnia but in some philosophical context, it could be likened to it.

Coming from a place of abundance means thinking of yourself as a person who already has everything he needs within him/her/hermaphrodite self. Coming from abundance means you do not leech value off others because you have no value for yourself. Instead, you come into the world looking to provide value.

Coming from abundance means being generous because you are so content with yourself that you are able to give to others from a full cup, because in abundance, in complete acceptance of yourself however you are, your cup is always full and never half-empty.

You, my dear, will always know your cup is full and in a state of abundance because you have values that keep you upright as well as boundaries of what you will and will not tolerate from yourself and others. Coming from a deep abundance means you have made the terms and conditions for your life and signed that damned contact in blood. With this newly-found abundance and your need for validation relinquished you'll realise your mood isn't so easily affected.

Have you ever realised how big an influence seeking approval has on your mood? And when you get it, it's similar to a hit of heroin—just a dirty high that lasts a couple of seconds and then sends you off sniffing for more approval.

Yes, dumb-dumb, you're basically a drug addict, or worse, a self-obsessed person on Instagram twenty-four-seven, which is fine because I am here to save you. Well actually, I'm not. I am here to show you how to save you and then it's up to you to put your own pants on. The key words here are UP TO YOU.

Wanting validation turns you into a piece of shit. Now you're thinking 'Why is being liked and approved of by other people going to turn me into a piece of shit?' I'm glad you asked, dumb-dumb, because your validation high is based on people being compliant to you and, in a more vain perspective, people feeding your ego.

Notice how people bend to the will of just the taste of some validation and you will realise how important it is to love yourself. When your self-esteem is self-generated, all the validation in the world could be given to you and it doesn't affect you in the way validation seekers are affected. It's taken and noted but it doesn't add anything to your already amazing self. Your ego is no longer flared by a compliment from a stranger. It's accepted with humility.

You're a step above now, conscious of what fills your mind and what's exuded through your body language. In kindness, you say thank you and it is instead used to fill your cup so you can give value to others. It is not used as gossip to make yourself seem like some hot shot starving for a compliment and then telling everyone about it when it does finally happen.

You no longer need the compliments so the universe gives you more love and validation than you can ever imagine because you are now the kind of person who can deal with this type of responsibility. The universe will always give you what you deserve, not what you need. This is precisely why the rich do not have to tell you they are rich, the confident do not have to tell you they are confident, but the desperate can be smelt from miles away and everyone runs from them. Why? Because they smell like shit.

Were all so desperate to be understood,
we forget to be understanding.

Beau Taplin

12. WHERE ARE THE DESPERADOS?

Attachment tends to inspire desperate and needy behaviour. If these attributes were humans, they would be considered a polyamorous relationship, but not the hot kind. They would be the gross, excessive public displays of affection, crazy running-up-and-down-the-street-at-three-am couple who everyone in the street hates. No one wants to be in the middle of this couple but if you are, you will be dragged down into the depths of insecurity, and of all human characteristics insecurity will have no mercy on the devil you will become.

Insecurity will rob you of your self-respect. It will rob you of a willingness to do things to please yourself and only yourself. It will also ruin the majority, if not all the relationships you can have because you're not sure of anything or anyone. Most importantly, you are not sure of yourself.

Can you see how and why you could be your own worst enemy? There's an old African proverb that states if there is no enemy within, the enemy outside can do no harm. It's an inability to have faith in who you are as an individual that causes this enemy within. The doubts you have in your mind will weaken it, along with the fear and conditioned thoughts that too many of us are subjected to, depending on our upbringing.

We are commonly told that we should always stay and fight, that is the noble thing to do, the 'right' thing. Although depending on the circumstance, if placed in a situation that is toxic, abusive and truly miserable, do you have enough self-respect and walk away when the situation is no longer tolerable? All the power in the world is absolutely useless if you cannot exercise it.

If there is a more crucial skill to hone, it's the ability to exercise the power of self-mastery. If you ever stopped to wonder, which sadly, many of us don't, you'll come to know that it's not by mere coincidence that many of the most prevalent religions around the world base most of their rituals around the execution of self-mastery. There is merit in it.

Do you have any idea what fasting does to your mind, body and most importantly, your soul? If you think the act of fasting is just starving yourself, then you are mistaken. When you forbid yourself from having something that your whole body desires, when you then tell your body that you can have it, you develop self-control and refine the skills to master your ability to control your desires. Temptation knocks but it no longer knocks with the same force, as you are a strong solid oak door now and you will and cannot be shaken or taken down as easily.

This is not to say go ahead and start fasting, it's just an example of how you can attain self-mastery and self-discipline, dumb-dumb, a shadow among the millions of ways. As always, everything here and in life is to be taken with a large slap of humour. Oh and please for everyone's sake if you have a chip that sits nicely on your shoulder, let that shit go, and no I won't even explain why you should. Just trust me.

If you're thinking where do you begin, self-mastery starts with a bigger purpose in mind but, most importantly, a solid sense of independence and, as stated previously, a silent mind for presence to take hold. All your desperate measures can be concluded when you're not so desperate to get to tomorrow instead of enjoying today, or right now.

It might be best to start with the question, 'Who am I and what am I doing here?' If you don't want to answer that and would like to continue being a lazy directionless sloth, then you best remove yourself from the Earth so that you're making less of a carbon footprint. At least you'll be contributing to less shit being put into Mother Nature.

So what is your true north? It doesn't haven't to be some whimsical display of 'saving all the children in the world from poverty' type ordeal. It can be as simple as that you want to go with the flow of life. Even if you want to be the best worker at Hooters, make that your vision. For Christ's sake, even if you want to get a degree in ant farming, then bloody well make that your vision.

Just pick something bigger than just focusing on how you feel or on your partner.

Don't get me started on making your partner your life's purpose. They'll resent you, wipe their feet on you, and my favourite, probably cheat on you multiple times. Don't be sad about it either, because a person with no purpose or vision is usually someone who is spineless. A spineless person generally has no respect for themselves, so your partner won't respect you. Usually, if a partner doesn't respect you, they'll either leave you or cheat, depending on how much money you have.

So if you don't want that shit to happen, pick something, dumb-dumb. It's fine if you change your vision, just refine it as you grow; nothing in life is absolute. Only you can decide what is important, only you can decide what becomes your reality and, most importantly, only you can decide your fate. You must contribute to life and you must feel as though you do, in whatever mediocre way.

It doesn't mean that you should treat your partner as though he or she is nothing. It means pick something outside of loving them because the last thing anyone wants is their partner breathing on their face with big obsessive bug eyes asking, 'What are you thinking about?' No, just no.

Let it be that your mission is to be the most devoted father or mother. You have a focus, a goal to strive for bigger than just yourself, and it is not enmeshed in your partner's mind and thoughts. You are your own individual self with your own goal and your partner can be his or her own individual self. You can then come together as two whole individuals that bring so much more to the table.

You have to develop self-mastery, to develop a spine, to create boundaries, to create great emotions, to create a fulfilling life.

Disclaimer—it's never certain if your partner will or won't cheat on you but having a purpose will make it less painful if they do because you have something else to focus on while you heal. There can be positives in all the pain. Let's be clear here—less likely doesn't mean that the impossible can't happen, dumb-dumb. Your best bet is to be able to screen people and qualify them.

Care about what others think and you
will always be their prisoner.

Lao Tzu

13. SCREENING FOR THE HOT STUFF CIRCLE

You need to qualify to be in your circle, because your circle is the hot stuff circle, much like an exclusive club, or better yet, Harvard. This is how you should let people be a part of your life, given that you provide enough value, are self-sufficient and don't need anyone. You choose to have them in your life.

Neediness will always send people running because it makes surrounding individuals feel trapped and anxious, and whoa my chest is getting really tight and I can't voice why you're bothering me SO GODDAMN MUCH. Just get the hell away from me, will you?

When you're needy even your presence is bothersome. In your mind you know you're bothering them and, as that self-fulfilling prophecy goes, you are what you think you are, which, in this case, is a pain in the backside. This is precisely why you need to get your mind right, have a bigger purpose and mission in life, and know what you want out of it.

Knowing what you want allows you to screen the worthy and unworthy individuals who will help you reach your life's mission. The consequences of allowing anyone and everyone in your life without qualifying them or screening their personality means that you're likely to make your life harder than it should be, and you'll essentially end up wasting a lot of your precious life and increase your chances being lied to, backstabbed, cheated on or abused. How fun.

Let me also make it clear—just because the individual is delicious-looking doesn't mean they have an amazing personality. You can chocolate coat shit, so stop screening people with your sex drive. Or do; it's your life, and these are your choices. If you want to subconsciously attract stage five clingers, then be my guest. Or you could just take two steps back and figure out whether or not this person is worth your time.

Similarly, just because someone likes you does not mean you should like them back and vice versa. There has to be a little more backbone to you because not just anyone will do. Well, let's hope not anyone will do, that is, if you're after a successful, rich, fulfilling life. If that's not what you are after, then you can go ahead and get freaky with the next crackhead walking your way. They'll probably treat you better than the Tinder lover with commitment issues.

For a truly quality life, you must be and want quality and it must be on win/win basis, that is, there must be mutual benefit for both parties if you decide you want to join each other's lives. However, to have this healthy relationship with anyone in life you must no longer be independent, that is fully self-sufficient, successful in your own virtue, and happy alone.

Once you think you have mastered independence then you can shuffle on up the love chain to interdependent where the keys are understanding, open communication and synergy between the couple. Gaining an appreciation of yourself must come first before sharing yourself with another, otherwise, you will have no clear identity and your partner and you will become disgusting mooches who will most probably become fat, complacent and have no sexual polarity.

Put it this way, dumb-dumb, have you ever known anything to be built and lasting without first having an extremely solid foundation? No, anything that's built like shit will fall to shit, so if you think you can have a lasting relationship of any sort without first working on making your foundation rock solid, centred in your core principals, a healthy social life and friends other than your partner (your mum doesn't count), then you can kiss any healthy, value-providing, nourishing relationship goodbye.

You and the partner will crumble to shit when the sun isn't shining in your direction, and for God's sake, if that does happen, avoid becoming the clingy dependant. Free yourself and the captive. You could forget about the pain of your wife leaving you for about twenty seconds by sleeping with the twenty-one-year-old bartender, but just as you try and tell yourself to look away from Kylie Minogue in her gold short shorts singing *Spinning Around*, it'll slap you harder when it comes full circle.

So deal with it. Deal with the things that bother you, deal with the terrible relationship with your partner, deal with the fact that you have problems being vulnerable, deal with the fact that you might not like the way you look in the mirror and the person you have become today. Do not avoid it. Deal with any issue you would usually whine about to your friend, and please, till the end of your time on this earth, work on your bloody self. As Stephen Covey says, 'The most important ingredient in any relationship is not what we say, or what we do, it's what we are.' So what are you, dumb-dumb?

Sometimes it's not always straightforward, but it's
not always confusing either. You just have to respect
a person's decisions without disrespecting them.

Temitayo Olami

14. YOUR OPINION SUCKS

Opinions are a great thing to have and it's always been said that if you stand for nothing then you will fall for anything, which, you guessed it, is a bad thing. But what about when you are listening to someone's opinion and you take it straight to heart?

You, my dear dumb-dumb, better hope you are not one of those people because it's basically like a horse trying to convince you it's a lion. You would never listen to that but, for some reason, we do it all the time.

That statement in itself is obviously not black and white and, without a doubt, there are things that should not be compromised such as being unmoving towards the evil of mass genocide based on ethnicity or religion, on Donald Trump being elected as president and whether or not pineapple should be on pizza.

Now hear me out here, loud and clear—having opinions is almost never the problem. The problem arises when you cannot deal with other people disagreeing with your beliefs which triggers your big fat ugly ego.

Now listen to me once again, loud and clear—whether or not you think you are right or wrong in regard to your opinion, everyone is entitled to their own opinion. No matter how racist, how egotistical, how morally incorrect, they have their own right to think and believe whatever they want. All you can do is either acknowledge them, respect them or even admire them. Then, in a conversational manner, if invited, state your opinion as to why you either agree, disagree or find merit in certain opinions. If they feel like taking on board what you have offered, that is fine. If they do not agree and do not wish to consider what you have said that is also okay. That's where it stops.

You do not need to take on their opinion like it's gospel and if you do, step back and remember that you are also an individual and you too have your own opinions. The primary cause of hate and chaos is in individuals fully expecting other individuals to believe and agree with everything they do and say, or better yet taking other each other's opinions to heart. Then what's left? I'll kill you, I'll beat you up, I'll blow up your entire country and, my favourite, I'll wipe you out as a race.

Does anyone ever think, well jeez, isn't that a little full on? Or is it an 'if you can't beat them join them' mentality that has individuals thinking inhuman actions can be justified based on a disagreement of belief or opinion? Now, dumb-dumb, I know you're thinking that you would never commit inhumane actions based on your individual opinion, that's extreme- which is true. However, I have seen friends stop being friends on the basis of one liking a Netflix drama series that the other one did not.

Petty opinions still invite ruin when accompanied by an unwillingness to listen, acknowledge or even just walk away. For God's sake, don't allow yourself to be so easily pushed off balance. Do not allow whatever is expressed around you to freely flow within your mind, body and heart without your damn permission to do so, damn it.

Yes, I said your permission because, as I have continuously stated, you are the captain of your own ship so you should not be surprised if your ship sinks from the hole that you, my friend, have created. The hole is a symbolic chink in your armour—a hole in your individuality, which is on you.

So grow a goddamn backbone, dumb-dumb, because this world is harsh and, as the great Rocky Balboa says to his son when he was being a pansy, 'You let people stick a finger in your face and tell you you're no good and when things got hard, you started looking for something to blame like a big shadow. The world ain't all sunshine and rainbows. It's a very mean and nasty place, and I don't care how tough you are, it will beat you to your knees permanently if you let it.'

But hold on- what about when you have a genuine opinion and someone knocks it off like it's garbage and all you want to do is throw them in the garbage? You guessed it—that's a no from me. Your opinion may seem like gospel to you and they may be an idiot for not wanting a bar of your amazing words of wisdom, words that could potentially change their life for the better, but your words and opinions are not gospel for anyone else unless they choose it to be.

If someone does take on what you are saying, it could well be the people who are obsessed with you, people in your cult (yes, you have a cult), and people who can't think for themselves- oh and there's also that odd case where another sound intellectual finds some meaning to your gospel and a beautiful discussion can occur between the two of you. But in any given case, violence and intolerance of each other's differences of belief and opinion is never the answer. So just be humble, dumb-dumb, live and let live, and have some trust that everyone knows what they're doing to some degree, even idiots.

We tend to project out of our own autobiographies what we think other people want or need to gratify our ego because maybe you've experienced what they're going through first-hand and you know what's best for them so they best listen, right? Wrong, dumb-dumb. Does that hurt? I hope so, so for the love of anything worth loving put that damn ego to sleep, because all it ever does is micromanage you and others. If you want people to run for the hills after conversing with them, you go ahead and behave that way, but don't say I didn't tell you so when you're a lonely old sod, dumb-dumb.

"Don't trust everything you see…
Even salt looks like sugar."

Maryum Ahsam

15. WHY SHOULD I TRUST YOU?

But wait, do you even know what it means to trust? You're thinking, 'Sheesh, trust who?' They're all animals out there. I've only got myself.'

Trust is the ability to live with what you do not know. How does that statement sit with you, dumb-dumb? What's that? No, I can't deal with that, I need to know everything?

There's a common belief that everyone is out to get you and no one is actually nice unless you fulfil some need of theirs. This is true to some degree, judging from recent catastrophic events the world is pointing out to us that everyone is out to get everyone, so the reasonable way to deal with this is that we should all hold a knife real close so we can stab people before they stab us.

What a wonderful world we live in. I don't know about you, but boy, that really helps me sleep well at night. I know all too well the many stories people have that give them a very good reason to not trust people. It's understandable—people can be savages and they can most definitely do all the lovely diabolical things that you least expect them to do—and for some dark, twisted reason it generally comes from those you trust the most—family, our lovers, best friends and the dearest co-workers who are bloody well not so dear anymore.

My argument to allow trust to flourish seems to be on the downhill here and it is. The basis of any strong relationship has long been said to be trust but it takes two separate individuals with their own inner power to come together to form the trust, and that power begins from within.

If you're aware of who you are, what your good at and what you're not good at, if you're able to see how emotions govern your life, if you can learn what your weaknesses are and how to control them to the best of your ability or even to just have an awareness of them, slowly, through this process of beginning to know who you are and understanding other people and how they operate so that you don't make stupid mistakes in life, you can increase that margin of emotional control just that little bit more until you become a person of power. In this power we observe more, investigate more, learn more, and this is how you get to know the people you intend to spend your time or even the rest of your life with. With this you can be bravely vulnerable and not get trampled on- because you're not stupid and you're about more than just being caught up your emotions.

The social normality nowadays has conditioned us to believe we should give trust openly and blindly, without discernment. I know you're thinking—'Yeah, that's great, but I've closed myself off from trusting and I just want to know how to open myself up again.' well, dumb-dumb, you don't. I also know this goes against everything we're encouraged to do but hear me out.

Did you know being trusting is a fairly new concept? It isn't always looked at as a good thing. If we look at ancient texts of the bible, in John 2:24 it says, 'But Jesus did not entrust himself to them'. Jesus did not trust himself to the hearts of men.

Whether you believe in Jesus or not is not the point. This text represents the idea that humankind is indecisive, ever-changing and their hearts may mean what they say in one moment but can easily change in another moment. This doesn't mean they were not truthful in the moment they made a vow, promise or an agreement. However, outside that moment is where everything gets blurred.

Essentially, to trust is to be cursed, because you can never be sure of anyone's real thoughts or feelings unless you are them or a mind reader, and I'm yet to meet a mind reader, so don't be a smartarse and just listen.

The idea here isn't to not trust at all, instead, think twice about who you give your trust to. Do they deserve it? Are they worth it? Have they shown qualities like someone with moral fibre and backbone? These are reasons to give trust. So when someone talks a big game are they just low-hanging fruit? And what's with all the flattering words?

Even still, in the back of your mind, be aware that they can still betray your trust, even though you've done all your discerning homework. Humans are unpredictable, fallible and… well, only human. But continue forward. However, being aware will make sure you're not brought to your knees if it ever does happen.

If you think a reason such as he's my uncle or she's my mum's best friend, or he's my teammate is a good enough reason to trust them, think again. Be the caveman you are and use your natural instincts—listen to your gut, use your intuition and your wit to determine for yourself who is actually worth your time, effort and trust. Your time on this earth is like sands in the hourglass, so make it worthwhile.

Longed for him. Got him. Shit.

Margaret Atwood

16. CONTINUOUS DISAPPOINTMENT

As the great Tyler Durden says, 'It's only after we've lost everything that we're free to do anything'.

If you look at your life now, you'll come to realise that everyone essentially follows the same path—birth, life, death. Some of us live longer, but no matter how long we live, we will eventually die.

Even if you lived to 700, in the timeline of the Earth that's nothing. So you might want to stop taking yourself so seriously and live your life with some authenticity and truth. For Christ's sake, just be real for bloody once, and let it happen while you're still breathing. Don't do it moments before your death when you realise that you put yourself through a lot of bullshit for no damn good reason. That is if you get the chance to ponder anything before death and your head isn't blown off instead, which would be bad luck.

Life has a dreamlike quality. Your memories are bullshit, your accomplishments are bullshit, the match you lost and are angry over is bullshit, that bullshit ego is bullshit. It's funny how people get on the bandwagon of bullshit. Unless you have found some nobble people who support you unconditionally, people are generally in your life and on your side until they're not.

People are drawn to those who reinforce their shitty degenerate behaviour. You're addicted to your thoughts and the problems in your thoughts, and that's essentially keeping you in a loop.

When you have trauma, you look for reasons to repeat those traumas unless you ascend. If you're not ready to go up, then you will stay in that snakeskin that wants to shed so badly, but it's too comfortable in there and shedding scares you because enduring pain is required to shed. Everything you really want is passing barriers and leaving the old skin behind.

So tell me this- how many of your actions are pushing your life forward? Pessimism is fine if you use it strategically but, for the most part, I can accurately guess that you're completely asleep just looking around on your mediocre horse and judging others.

Also, if you think this whole idea of 'I'll be happy when I achieve A or B', then you will continuously be disappointed. Only when you're not stuck in an outcome will you learn true freedom from disappointment. You ask, 'How the hell do I do that?' The only way is to keep your internal chatter still long enough to smell the roses. The idea of zen came from a Buddhist monk who stood in front of his students, held up a flower and stared at it. Funnily enough, only one of his students resonated with the teaching.

If you don't get it, then let me spell it out for you, dumb-dumb, we are put on this earth to engage, not to disengage. The monk was teaching complete engagement in the moment.

Know this—we don't take action from presence, we take action when we are present. So learn to be present. Give yourself and others the respect of being in the moment with them. Don't half-arse your moments thinking of things that are not surrounding you, engage fully in your present moment and feel your body.

Stop trying to orchestrate everything and let go of outcomes. Then, and only then, will you be able to take each moment for what it bloody is—a second closer to your untimely and possibly miserable death.

As you want people to place importance in the things that interest you, show that same interest back. As the old Chinese proverb states, always give before you receive. You will increase your emotional bank account with whoever you wish to have a strong relationship with, and yes- an emotional bank account is exactly what you think it is, I hope.

Consider your life as a transaction between you and others—some are balanced, some are overdrawn and some are in excess from one side and not the other. If you treat your interactions with the people you give a damn about in a balanced way, or if you just want to be considered a half-decent human being, then note the kinds of transactions you make with these people. You'll know when you've overdrawn because they will be irritated by you and they walk the other way when they see you in plain sight. If you valued your worth, you would do exactly the same.

So be considerate of what you ask of yourself and of others, and consider the disadvantage it is to you. Rethink your relationships, and if you've overdrawn one too many accounts, you'll come to see why your family members no longer want to be near you or even some of your closest friends, and vice versa. When they irk you to no end, it is likely because they require much more than they are prepared to give, and you know that instinctively and you don't like it one single bit.

So what do you do? Consider your accounts, rewire your habits of consciousness to better yourself, and live presently. Then you will give more of yourself to others effortlessly because by living presently, you give others the space to speak and be heard without judgement, just understanding and pure present concentration.

The most valuable thing in life is to be acknowledged fully, to be heard, but not always to fix things, even if you do have all the answers. And please, oh please, never neglect small courtesies and kindnesses. They will forever get you what you want from the adult children that roam the earth, dear dumb-dumb.

I love my rejection slips. They show me I try.

Sylvia Plath

17. REJECTING ME SOFTLEY

Dumb-dumb, there's no easy way to take rejection, especially when that beautiful someone has you so hooked. What's even more impressive is that they're giving you next to nothing and you, my sweet thing, are dedicating all your energy, time and attention to this individual in the hope of recapturing a sweet moment in time that entangled you both.

Do you think that sweet blissful moment you shared can be recaptured? I mean, surely if it happened once it can happen again, right? Those feelings they made you feel, the way you touched each other and stared into each other's souls; it was no lie.

But then you took it and ran like a maniac with no self-control, and you imagined in that moment that this was the person of your dreams and that he or she would solve all the cracks of your life with the oozing juices of the esoteric love you shared.

Even if it only happened once and never again, and even though they have been dodging and weaving your every advance since that moment, you are bracing your veins for a hit of that trip down memory lane to that brief moment in time that keeps you yearning for them to love you the way you want them to love you, right?

If only he or she were loving me like I should be loved, then all these obsessive, self-doubting, image-contorting feelings would stop arising. They clearly can't see how happy you could make them. It's at this point you realise you should make them see how they should want you just as much as you want them.

Maybe if you accidentally walk past their work they'll remember. No, so you stalk their Instagram story and bump into them wherever they are. And their friends will love you? No, you'll go one better and flood them with messages about how you truly feel with your raw untamed emotions. With all the force of your obsessive love, you explain in disgusting detail how you were meant to be together forever like Romeo and Juliet. You'll quote 'a thousand times the worse to want thy light' and, with that sophisticatedly crass vomit of words, surely then they'll see you are the right one for them.

It's long been said that if you need to force a fart it's probably shit, and that magnificent quote is applicable to all areas of life. You can orchestrate a number of things, but it only accounts for material things. The real things in life such as love, trust and relationships cannot be orchestrated if you want them to be pure and meaningful.

Your intention and socially constructed assumptions to situations gives you your appropriate outcome. You will get the appropriate outcome, not the one you want, but the one you need. However, it is almost never in your hands when you are dealing with other people.

Never force anything, because when you use force the adverse happens. That is the law of nature. Don't ask me why, it's just how shit works.

If you're forcing a relationship, it will never work. If you force your friend to meet with you even though they don't want to, you'll push them away.

Forcing means to show how much you want to be near them, and it shows how much you want to make them do what you want with no regard for them. Ultimately, it shows how insecure and inconsiderately needy you are.

Forcing carries so much negativity and aggression that the gentle souls you wish to persuade will be so put off by you and you'll end up one lonely little critter and for good reason.

The very nature of force entails neediness, which means you lack, which means you don't muster up in the caveman food chain so that your genes will be passed on, which means you get passed on, or better yet, passed by.

The forcing nature also means that you get angry and resentful when they don't respond or don't want a bar of what you have to offer, so you offer two bars, which makes things worse.

My dear dumb-dumb, it is only when you live your life without wanting anything from others that you will find everything you've yearned for, for it magically appears.

It's best that you work on yourself at every opportunity and find that everything you need is always within you. You are not lacking. work on developing the tools to make yourself self-sufficient and ensure that your presence around others adds value because, as the great Jim Carrey says, 'The greatest currency in this life is the effect you have on others.'

Everyone enters and exits the world the same way, but they leave different marks behind. What valuable mark will you leave behind in this world?

When the ego dies, the soul awakes.

Mahatma Gandhi

18. GIVE ME AN 'E' FOR EGO

Has a humiliating situation ever occurred and left you brewing angrily over what you should have said, what you should have done? All the while your blood pressure is through the roof and your thoughts make Darth Vader look like an angel.

No one else is burning. You're burning a hole in your own mind and putting yourself through all this pain, my dear dumb-dumb, and the perpetrators are fast asleep, not giving a rat's arse.

In what way does this brewing and grudge-holding serve you? It really doesn't. You need to be aware of your ego at this point and realise how much you have to feed it for it to stay alive and burning. If you're conscious of not playing to your ego's thought games you might be able to express what needs to be expressed and then move on.

You must feel your emotions fully, otherwise they arise as knots and other symptoms in your body, so express and let go. However, do it in the moment or when you are alone. Do not hold onto unnecessary burdens that will weigh down your life.

Learn not to engage with the silly egotistical thoughts you have swimming around like sharks in your head. You'll know true peace when you can disengage from your thoughts and just feel and be present in the moment.

But how do you achieve this? It takes two things. The first is insight—the ability to focus completely on what is happening in the moment, and surrender—letting go of all arising thoughts.

So if you're having either good or bad thoughts let them all go, stay out of your mind and just be conscious of everything without thinking or over-analysing. In the thinking moments, you will get trapped in your head and create emotions and reactions that trigger you.

Just like anything else, you must train yourself in this and you must unlearn the years spent identifying with the noise in your mind and considering yourself one with your thoughts.

Know this, dumb-dumb, you are not your thoughts and your thoughts are not you. They are a reaction to your disease within your environment. When your thoughts resist life, random and disturbing thoughts arise. When something happens to conflict with a belief, your mind is set on fire.

Your thoughts are merely an unconscious reaction to life, but they are not you and you would be wise not to consider them a part of your true nature. Those thoughts are your ego and the ego does not serve anyone but itself.

The ego will break you down to satisfy its needs. It will humiliate, abuse and seek constant validation in order to stay alive, and it will surely eat at your humble sense of self. You will never be satisfied with anything in life as long as you continue to identify with your ego and your thoughts, so be free and be willing to surrender to life and it will undoubtedly begin to slowly but surely surrender to you too.

Live for now, live for consciousness and no ego, comprende?

But how do we differentiate between the two? Consciousness comes from deep within the gut. It's quiet yet has a calming presence. The ego is diabolical and puts you on edge immediately.

If we could compare the ego to an individual it would be like your own inner Hitler or Stalin; an eccentric and tyrannical dictator. Isn't it terrible to think you could have something close to those psychopaths dictating a large portion of your life choices? It's all but selfishly ambitious and considers others a threat. If you are like this, you will never truly know peace.

So what are your options here? You can continue to have Hitler and Stalin rule your life or you can give your mind and that chip on your shoulder a rest. Live in service and contribution, give that ego a higher purpose, show a little sacrifice and, while you're at it, exercise some goddamn empathy, for Christ's sake.

Resolve to be thyself: and know, that he
who finds himself, loses his misery.

Matthew Arnold

19. JUST GO TO INDIA

All humans are run by energy. Fear, sorrow, happiness, sadness, excitement or anger. All these emotions are essentially energy that is focussed by you based on how you decide to express it, it is then transmuted into the world to achieve whatever outcome was intended, even though what was intended doesn't always play to our favour.

However, dear dumb-dumb, did you know that fear and sorrow inhibit action? It's best to transmute those feelings of fear and sorrow into an action that will benefit you. It takes less energy to do something that you like rather than one that pisses you off or keeps you in moody town.

Fear and sorrow puts people in the hospital. It keeps people asleep from living their potential greatness. It is lazy.

If your life is worth something, you'd do best not to entertain these emotions. Or you can, and you can be a whiney piece of shit and complain and feel sorry for yourself. In that case, don't even bother trying to befriend me because your lame excuse for a life is not something anyone with a passion to live wants to be surrounded by.

If you can manage to go one step further, if you can transmute emotion into happiness and develop the best damn sense of humour towards everything that comes your way, you'll live a fulfilling life. Humour, especially towards yourself, is a notable psychological trait and signifies true strength of character. It serves as a reminder to not take yourself or life so seriously and that nothing is ever personal.

Nothing ever stays the same. Everything is always changing and nothing can be grasped forever. We cannot escape this and, when we resist it, it persists. Surrender to control and never resist or identify with anything.

No one is better or less than anyone when you consider that we are born and die with nothing. You will find the moments enjoyed in the present and feeling the emotion of the moment will be the ones that bring the most happiness.

However, happiness is within you, and it's not something you search for externally. If you do that, you'll be searching for the rest of your life, dumb-dumb. So let's cut it short and save you the lifelong search of meditating in India for ten months eating nothing but lentils, by telling you that you will need to be the source of all your emotions. Everything else is fleeting and if you rely on the fleeting then you will be a temperamental piece of work.

However, maybe you should consider India. Go anywhere where everything you're accustomed to is taken away or is difficult to access as you try to 'find yourself'. You'll do superbly.

There's a reason why many individuals go to these places in order to find their peace or themselves, which is, in fact, the consciousness within themselves and disidentification from their Hitler ego.

But how, you ask? Well, dumb-dumb, when everything is taken away from you, you're forced to live in gratitude and realise how good you really have it. This brings supreme presence with the moment your in and a little something called humility begins to wrap its fingers around your hardened heart.

Tears may begin to flow, and you won't be able to help it as intense presence with your moment brings this on, as if you've been asleep your whole life. From that moment, you will know it doesn't matter where you are, as long as you are in the here and now. You will have found yourself and your discontentment will cease to exist.

Listen loud and clear, dumb-dumb, there is never nothing going on and there are no ordinary moments. Each second of your life is ever-changing and absolutely wonderful. Always be aware that a silent mind will lead to a content heart, for boredom and anxiety is of the ego.

So fear not. Life is but a ride. Do not resist. Just sit back and enjoy.

The best way to find yourself is to lose
yourself in the service of others.

Mahatma Gandhi

20. SENDING YOU OFF WITH LOVE

This is the end of the road for us, dumb-dumb. It's been lovely on my part being the mentor/offender. My hope is for you as an individual who's read too much, thought too little and have been personally afflicted with each of these lessons is that you find some sort of resonance with what has been expressed.

Yes, that's right. I was creepy. I was clingy. I was needy. I didn't want to stand up for my life or respect myself. I wasn't willing to serve anything (except for pancakes and only for myself). Oh, and ego. I had everyone covered for size in terms of how big that shield was. It covered a whole bunch of empty space. Instead, I filled that space with passion, compassion, vulnerability and empathy, and made myself a useful vehicle of presence to carry myself in the world.

Whatever you find that's useful in this book, if you find anything useful at all, please take it with a grain of salt and a generous serve of humour. However, if you have made it here, I win. But honestly speaking, this book is just a bunch of experiences and a journey of some sort.

Whatever journey you are on, and even if you're not and just think I'm hilarious (which is usually the case), it's best to know that the beauty of life is always in the journey. Rarely is the destination all it's cracked up to be. So go on lots of journeys and don't be impatient to reach the end. If you are, you'll miss all the best bits and you'll reach your destination feeling as though life passed you by.

You pay dearly when you give up your time to focus on issues that do not allow you to be of service to others. The shitty issues you have today keep you in a trance and keep you in your mind. If you want to keep sleeping, then do. Just don't expect me to sign your copy of the book, okay, honey?

Dear dumb-dumb, I just want to grab you, shake you and tell you to take your time with everything with everyone. Place your utmost focus on the moment because the only place you're rushing to as each day passes is your grave. With that in mind, you might want to pull the rein in on your horse. Reconsider what's most important to you. you never know when a truck's waiting to hit you.

It won't be easy, but it will be worth it. I love you, dumb-dumb.

www.ingramcontent.com/pod-product-compliance
Lightning Source LLC
Chambersburg PA
CBHW031301250726
48655CB00005B/2299